THE SUN!

A MY INCREDIBLE WORLD PICTURE BOOK

MY INCREDIBLE WORLD

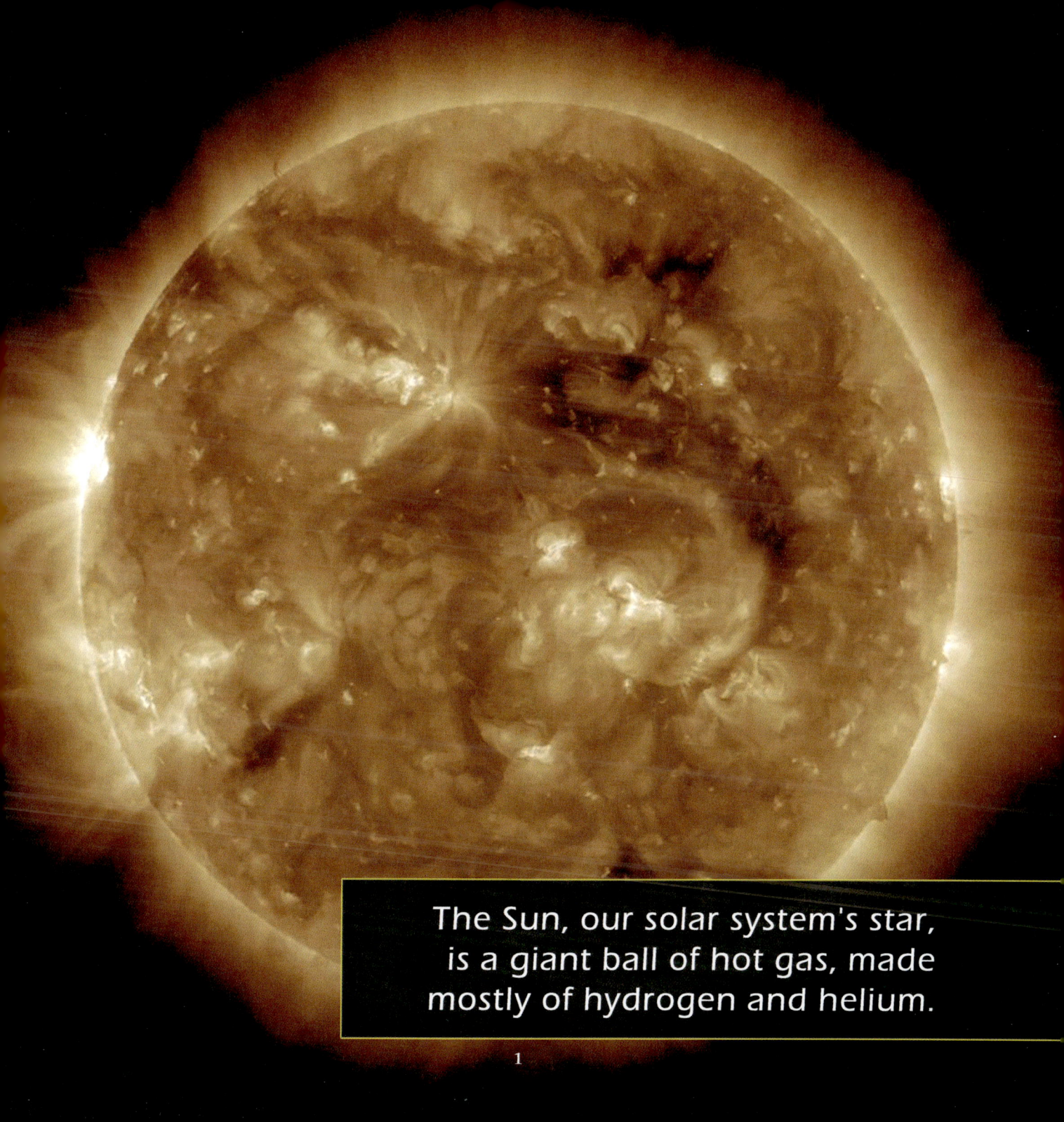

The Sun, our solar system's star, is a giant ball of hot gas, made mostly of hydrogen and helium.

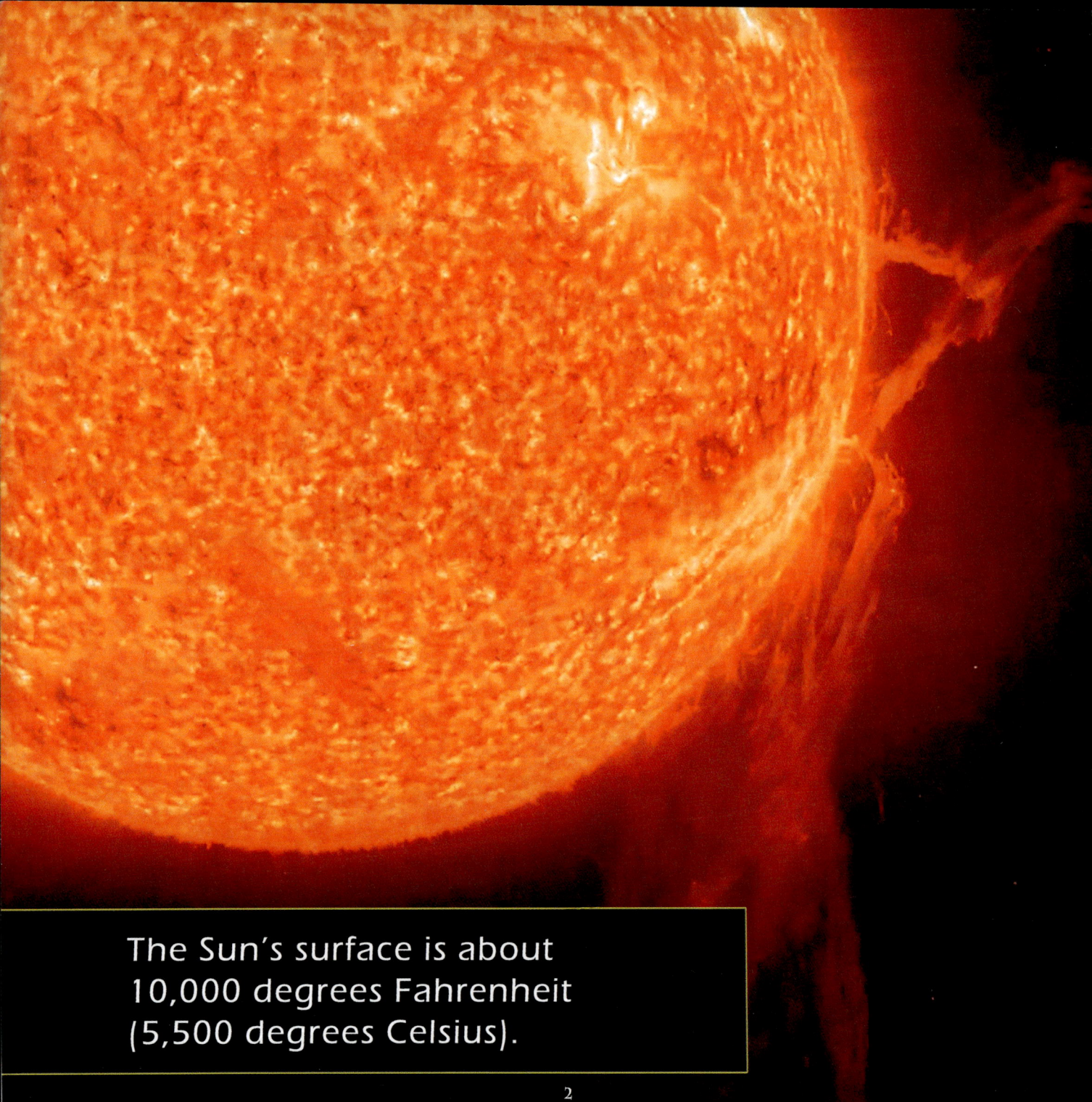

The Sun's surface is about 10,000 degrees Fahrenheit (5,500 degrees Celsius).

Its core is even hotter—reaching 27 million degrees Fahrenheit (15 million degrees Celsius)!

The Sun is around 93 million miles (150 million kilometers) away from Earth.

It takes the light from the Sun
about 8 minutes to reach us!

The Sun has been shining for
about 4.6 billion years.

It still has enough fuel to burn
for another 5 billion years!

The Sun is so big that you could
fit 1.3 million Earths inside it!

Even though it's huge, the Sun is considered a medium-sized star.

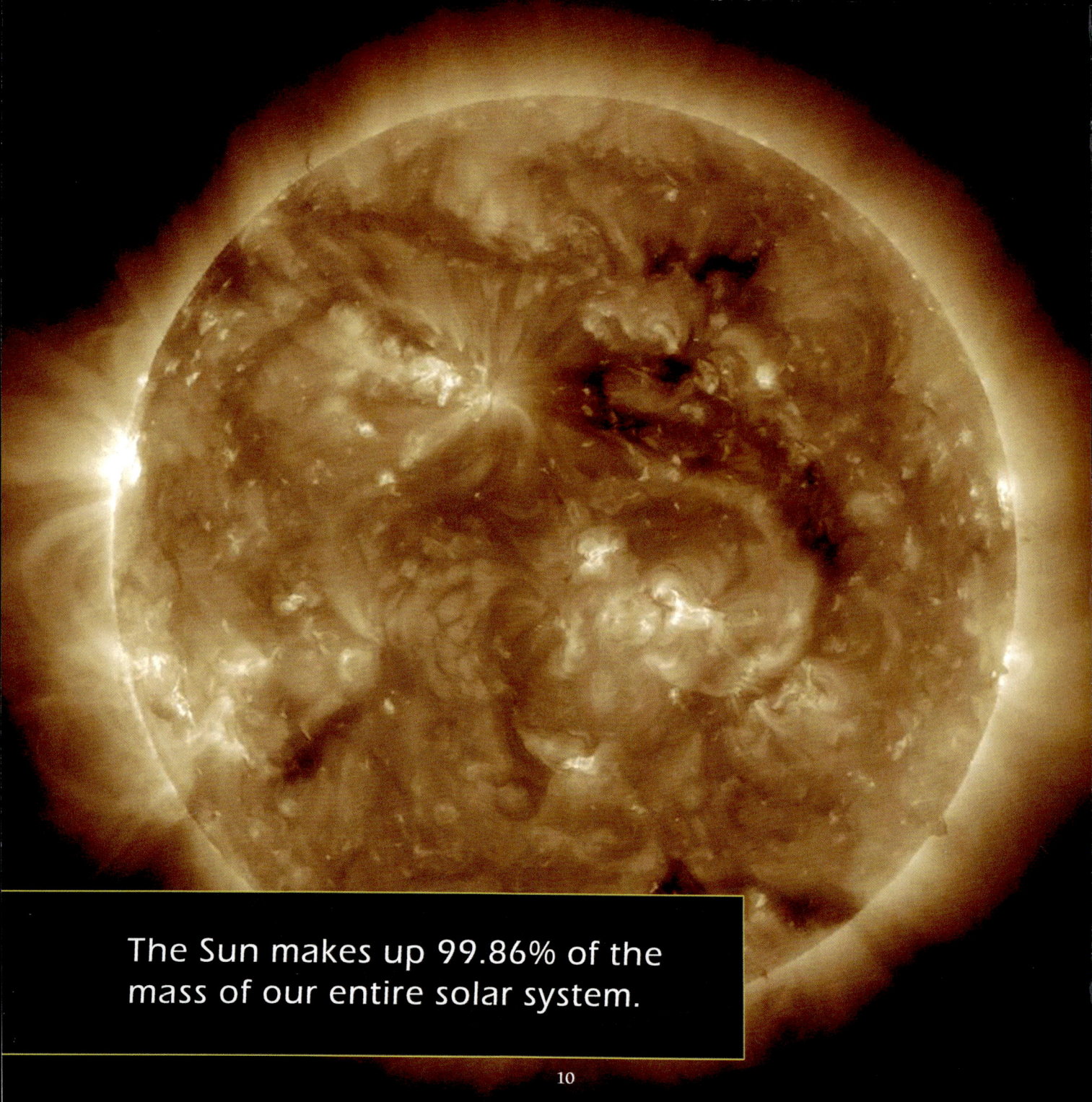

The Sun makes up 99.86% of the mass of our entire solar system.

It is one of more than 100 billion
stars in the Milky Way galaxy!

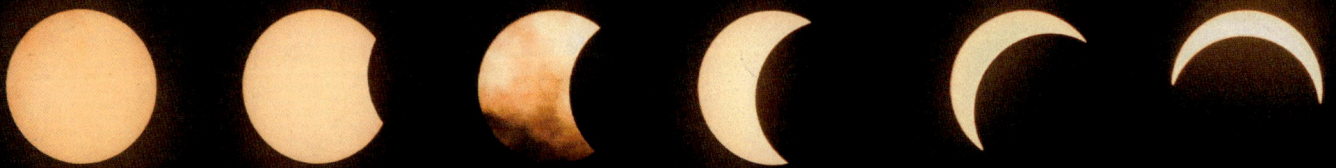

A **solar eclipse** happens when the Moon moves between the Sun and Earth, blocking its light.

During a **total solar eclipse**, the sky can get so dark it looks like nighttime, even during the day!

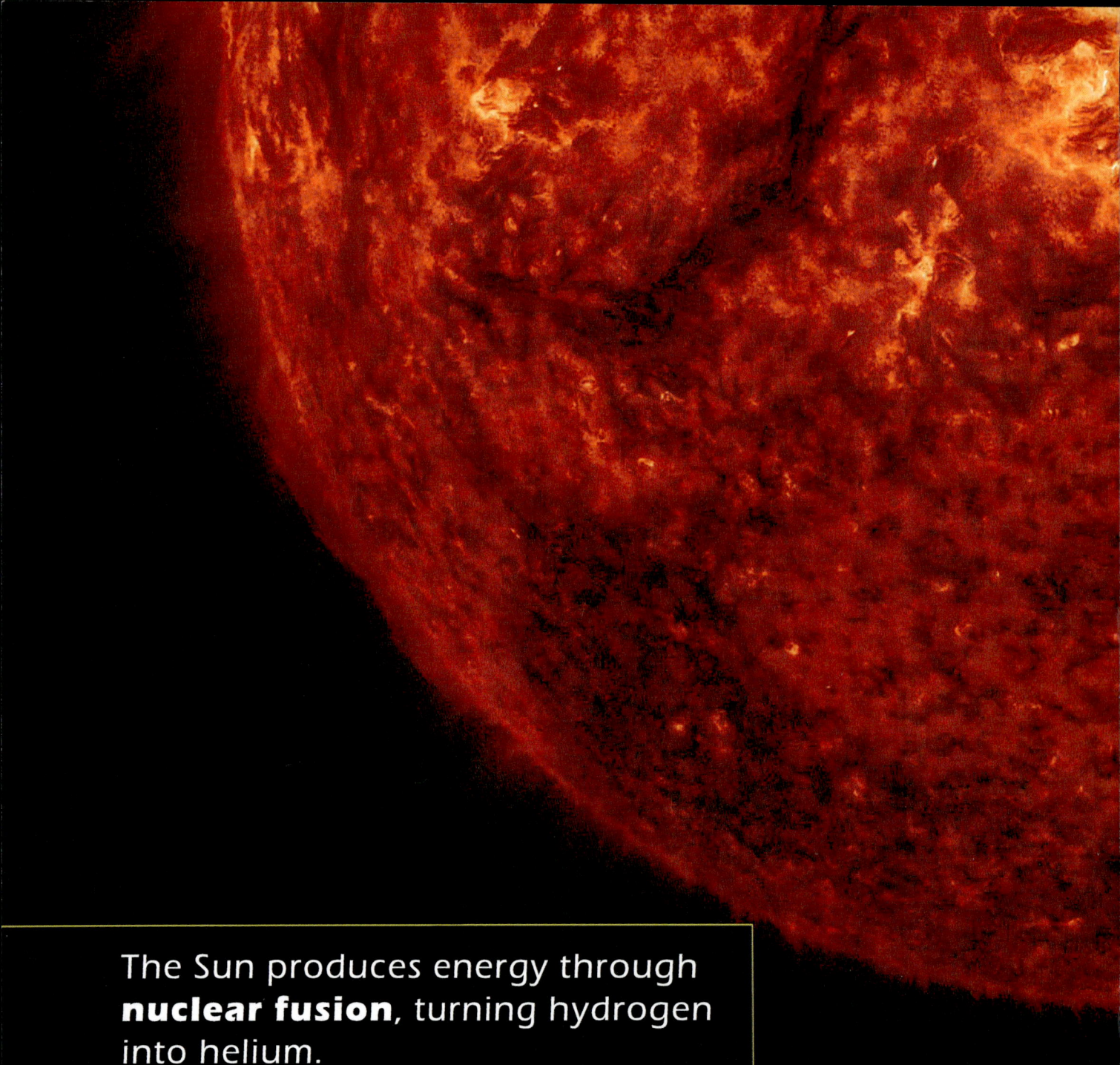

The Sun produces energy through **nuclear fusion**, turning hydrogen into helium.

This fusion process releases light, heat, and solar wind.

The Sun's magnetic field causes **solar storms**, which can create beautiful **auroras** on Earth.

Powerful **solar flares** from the Sun can disrupt satellites and power grids.

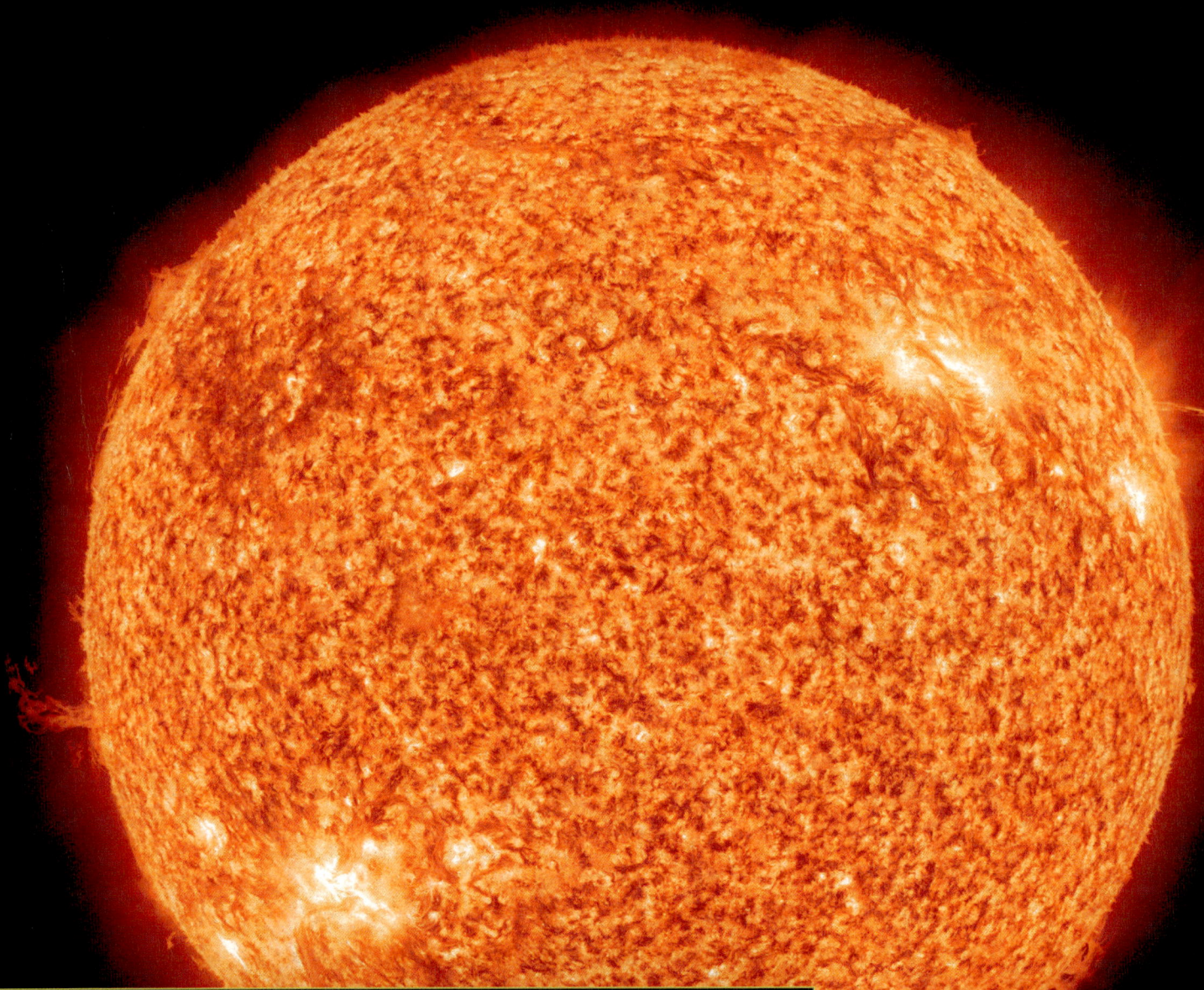

Every 11 years, the Sun goes through a **solar cycle**, with changing magnetic activity.

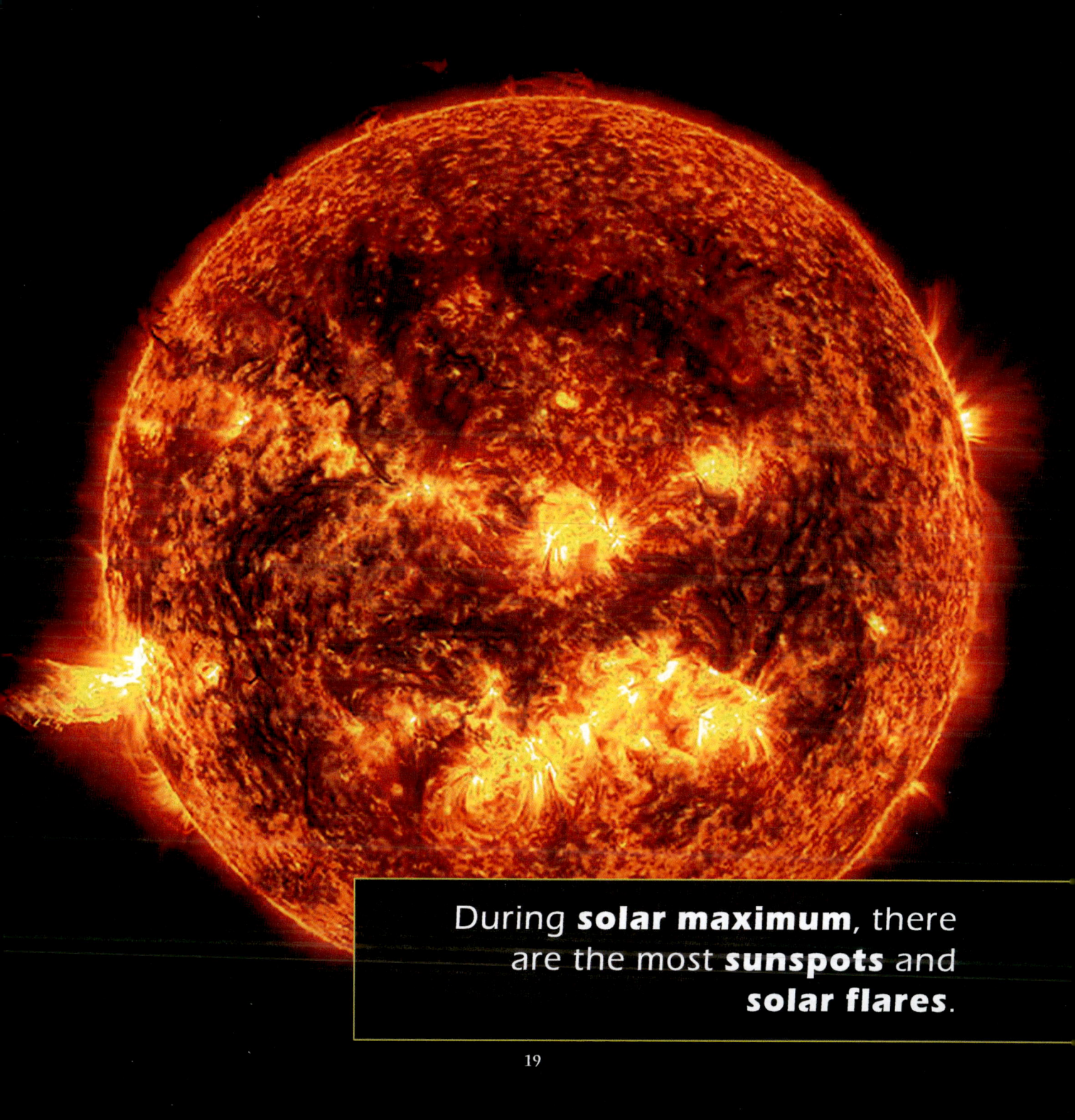

During **solar maximum**, there are the most **sunspots** and **solar flares**.

The Sun's gravity keeps all the planets, including Earth, orbiting around it.

Without the Sun's heat and light,
life on Earth wouldn't be possible!

The Sun is incredible!

Made in the USA
Coppell, TX
24 March 2025